ENDEX 2
UNCUT

Clive Ward

DEDICATION

A percentage of the proceeds from sales of this book will be donated to www.forgottenveteransuk.com my chosen charity.

ACKNOWLEDGMENTS

I'd like to thank my wife Elaine for editing the book and Antonella Caputo for her patience while proof reading it.

By Clive Ward

The Unnamed Soldiers
Army Barmy
Bumpers & Bed Blocks
EndEx
You Wouldn't Belize It
The Goat Killer
Homeless

Writing with E Ward

Half Day Closing
In Sympathy

FOREWORD

Thirty plus years later looking back, I have to admit my time in the army was some of the best years of my life. It wasn't because I liked it. There sure was nothing to like about losing comrades, missing loved ones, etc. I liked it because I was young, hungry and full of life. We all were, we were a brotherhood. Even though I didn't like some of those I served with, now I miss and love all of them living or taken away. Only those who've served will understand.

Here we go again, and here was me thinking I'd nailed most subjects in ENDEX ONE. Apparently not. Here are a few more give away signs you were once in the military plus a few memories along the way.

You know, I think I'm doing okay fitting into civilian life. I've rarely looked back. I was wondering though does anyone still bull their work boots? I've been bulling mine for the umpteenth time this week and I still can't get that finish I used to get. I can't find Dual or Seal to save my bacon anywhere in the shops.

I was also wondering if anybody else still makes a bed block before muster? It annoys the shit out of the missus. But I do give her a lay in on Sunday's till 0900 hours, and there's always a cup of NATO standard

1

and an egg banjo waiting for her downstairs to get down her face before we shoot off for church parade. Which reminds me, my hair needs cutting, three on top, one on the back and sides. This Civvy life is a doddle. I've completely broken free, but my missus is not so sure. Right, where's my mess tins I'm Hank Marvin, bacon grill for tea.

BACK TO BASICS

Choggie Burgers, Egg banjo's, the first fag after a BFT, the smell of Swarfega, reveille, standing orders, Gas, Gas, Gas. Isn't it strange how a few words can trigger a flashback, right back to the days of Blanco and carbolic soap for some. Looking back, I get enormous satisfaction from pretty much all of it. Those memories will never fade. Let me take you back to the beginning.

BASIC TRAINING

I can remember how nervous I felt on my first day. Being greeted at the guardroom and shown to my new accommodation, then finding out I was to share a room with fifteen other blokes for the next eighteen weeks. All I could hear was all these different accents from all over the country, Jocks, Geordies, Scousers, the Welsh, Irish, Brummie, Cockney, Mancunian, alien. Shit, I needed a translator and quick.

3

BUTCHERED

Then there was my first haircut. Once the hair was shaved away, that had buried our faces, suddenly everyone looked like a coconut and some looked like they should still be at school and there were a few who looked like they had escaped from the local mental hospital.

KIT ISSUE

We couldn't wait to be marched down to the QM stores, to be issued with our new kit. We wanted to look like our Sergeants and Corporals, but we ended up looking like we'd just been to rent a tent, everything was two sizes too big for us. I heard if your uniform fitted you, you could get discharged for being deformed. I couldn't believe it when I signed for my newly allocated SLR. The thing it was older than I was. That's nothing. When I got issued my 58 pattern webbing, I found out it was older than my Mum! I could fit the webbing belt around my waist twice.

What was next, a sun dial watch?

REVEILLE

After a night of pillow fights and all sorts of late night shenanigans, we were woken up at 0600 hours. That's when everything changed. Our Corporals, who were so nice to us when we first arrived, had turned into arseholes overnight. What was going on? They were handing out 100 decibel bollockings. Why were they being so mean? We soon realised that was fuck all to what was about to come our way.

With our KFS and mugs green in our left hand behind our backs, we proudly marched off to the cook-house for our first breakfast.

'Gents fall in, I'll march you to the cookhouse, saves you walking'

QUEEN'S PARADE

After taking our place in the long queue, we all wondered why it was taking so long for the queue to go down. Usually it was due to some slop jockey still half asleep, after getting up at 0400 hours, trying his hardest to keep up with the demand for egg banjos. Finally, we got inside. There's one thing you can say about the army, you always got a good breakfast. One sausage, one egg, one spoonful of beans or watery tomatoes and fried bread, all washed down with a large mug of sweet tea.

The problem was that there was never enough time in training to sit down relax and enjoy it. Before you knew it, you were being chased out of the cook-house by some Corporal you'd never seen before.

'I LEFT YOU IN THIS POSITION...'

It was time for our first taste of drill. Marching onto the parade square we didn't know what to expect. It wasn't long before we had an audience. As anyone who has served in the military knows, watching new recruits go through the first set of drill instruction was priceless, a sight to behold.

'Move along, gentlemen, you can always join them if you want' bellowed out our drill Sergeant. I'll always remember his name, Sergeant York of the Duke of Edinburgh Regiment.

I left you in this position, one-two-three, one-two-three, up-two-three, down-two-three, swing -two, three, about-two-three, in-two-three, out-and-shake-it-all-about. What was all that about? More bloody moves than celebrity come dancing. But when we got it together we were brilliant, or we thought we were, 'eft-ight, eft-ight.'

DID YOU KNOW?

There are many stories and myths associated with the Parade Ground. It's said within the British Army, that the Parade Ground holds a special symbolic representation of a sanctuary for a unit's fallen soldiers, and in line with this symbolism it is deemed 'hallowed ground' and is respected as such. The key to the square is always kept in the guardroom... allegedly!

OPEN WIDE

We now wanted to practice our drill every chance we got. On our way back from dinner, I remember everyone saluting the dentist on his way to the Med Centre and being happy when we got the drill movement right, up-two, three, down-two-three, swing. Everyone practiced their salutes on the dentist, an aging RAF officer, we nicknamed him TOPGUM. We used him as a sort of training aid, the poor bloke. He always gave one back and never gave you a mouthful when you got it wrong. I suppose he got the last laugh when you were lying back in his dentist chair. 'Remember me you little bastard, nurse pass me that extra-large drill, will you.'

I remember saluting the RSM once and suffering my first character assassination and trying not to well up from his barrage of abuse.

'Somewhere there is a tree working really hard to produce oxygen, so that you, sunshine, can breathe. Now go and fucking find it and apologise to it.'

BULLSHIT

Room jobs, area cleaning, buffing the accommodation floor with the bumper that weighed a ton for the first time, using that orange gunk floor polish. Blister's on top of blister's. Using Brasso on the radiator taps and door knobs to make them shine. Wire Wool on the washroom taps.

Then being taught how to burn your boots down to get rid of the pimples by heating a spoon over a candle. Followed by being shown how to bull them up, even our black PT shoes. And how to shrink that landing strip beret, hot water, cold water, hot water, cold water. Then putting it on the radiator to dry overnight, to wake up in the morning to find it's still the same fucking shape. Even though you convinced yourself it wasn't. And then, there were those mind boggling locker layouts, building bed blocks, and hospital corners, great fun.

After they'd taught you how to do all that, the next stage was they ripped you to shreds. Your kit went out of the window, beds and lockers destroyed on a daily basis for the first few weeks for no reason. Water bottles flying through the air were a common occurrence. Show parades in full number two dress, presenting the item you've been pulled up on, which could be anything from your best boots to your whole locker layout, this meant moving your whole locker down to the guardroom for 2200 hours. If you didn't pass inspection, you were back down there at 23.00 hours and every hour after until you passed. You had to give 110% at all times or the whole squad suffered.

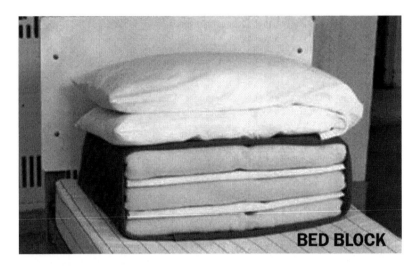

BED BLOCK

DOWN TEST AND ADJUST

Firing an SLR for the first time, was exciting, but a bit scary. There was always someone on the wrong gas setting, wrong sized butt, not holding their weapon properly, forgotten their ear defenders and couldn't shoot for toffee. Twenty rounds later, a cut eye, bruised jaw, ringing ears, he got it right in the end.

INTERVIEW WITHOUT COFFEE

You either developed that warped sense of humour or you gave up. In the first six weeks it was easy to get out, but after that you were fucked. The longer you stayed in, the harder it became to leave. Your only options were to do a runner and go AWOL, go down the guardroom pretending you were on a motorbike, with added sound effects (working your ticket) or to put in a PVR request, at a price of course. I remember the going rate in 1974 was around £400, about fifteen weeks wages.

If someone wanted to leave, the military would spend weeks trying to change the person's mind. When they'd finally accepted the application to PVR, the person concerned had to go on OC's then CO's interviews. They made it as difficult as they could for the person to get out. When they finally gave in and accepted that the person concerned wanted out, it was three to six months of hell waiting for their release date. Because then they were the guy who couldn't handle it.

FIELD CRAFT

Dash down, crawl, set your sights and fire. There was one member of our squad who previously worked for the Forestry Commission, during our first lesson on camouflage and concealment he turned himself into a bloody garden centre. There was that much greenery he looked like a bush.

TWO'S UP

Trying to stay awake during lectures was impossible. The punishment was usually twice around the block go, not fast enough do it again, get caught again, staff parade 22.00 hours.

Back then everybody smoked, if you didn't, then you had a serious passive smoking problem and a nicotine addiction, which made you start smoking anyway. I remember the five minute smoke breaks during lessons. When it was the day before pay day it was one fag between eight of you, two's up three's up four's up... last drags.

ALPHABETICAL ORDER

Standing in line waiting for my pay, it was always in alphabetical order, so I had lots of time to rehearse 'pay and pay book correct, sir!' Salute, about turn and march off smartly out through the door. If you got it wrong, staff parade 2200 hours. Once you got your measly sum, you were off down the NAAFI to blow it, the first chance you got.
It was funny watching the obliging NAAFI girls, the only girls you'd see on a regular basis for the next few months, get prettier and prettier.

The first thing I'd buy with my weeks wages £3.50 (after deductions) was a pint of milk, a pie and a chocolate cream éclair or something similar. Then in the Naafi shop to buy, boot polish, Brasso, chocolate, soap, toothpaste, razors, stamps and a pouch of baccy. By the time you got back to the block you were skint after paying the doubles back loan sharks.

TWICE AROUND MY BEAUTIFUL BODY GO

Who can forget the Stanley Matthews style blue shorts with starched creases down the front and back, that when they got wet reached down below the knees and the short sleeve PT white or red vests with the V shaped necklines.

That first BFT. The introduction to the assault course, now try it with a log! The Log race, steeplechase, stretcher race, milling, the rope climb... I hated that, pushups, pull ups, star jumps, suddenly you thought you were fit, you were superman. Then they'd break you again with five, ten and twenty mile runs. Then returning to barracks after a run, to fork left was to return to the gym and finish, whereas forking right meant a trip over the assault course. Now you were FUBAR. But as the weeks went by you felt yourself getting stronger and fitter, even though you smoked thirty fags a day. Trying to skive out of it was impossible, going sick was an obstacle course on its own, needless to say, only those who were about to receive the 'last rites' went sick.

SENNYBRIDGE

Then came the final battle camp, it lasted two weeks. For me it was Sennybridge in the Brecon Beacons. A cold, wet, windy festering shithole in the back of beyond, full of suicidal sheep that lay on the road at night waiting for speeding military vehicles. Shooting them on the live firing range was a rite of passage. It rained all year round there, the only plus side, the rain was warmer in the summer. I was there in February, wet feet for two weeks.

Sennybridge was the first time I heard the phrase 'Come on, it's just over that hill.' Most of the time if we weren't tabbing, we'd be hidden away in one of the many forestry blocks lying in our shell scrapes with our bond hooks, with just the horizon to worry about. Those rare moments of peace and quiet tucking into my tin of ham paste and hard tack followed by a Tiffin bar and boiled sweets, until the enemy orange forces decided to go and spoil it all by attacking us.

It was a heartbreaking, back breaking, soul breaking time, but if you came out the other side intact after hearing that magic word ENDEX you were ecstatic, you'd made it. You were happier than a belt fed weapon. Don't get a bag on, get a mag on and stag on.

DID YOU KNOW?

The war office obtained the Sennybridge training area in 1939. It is the third largest training area in Britain and covers an area of twelve miles by five miles. It's that desolate that nobody knows where it is. Sennybridge is the ideal training area as it can never be viewed from space because of the permanent cloud cover, i.e. It's always fucking pissing it down.

THE BIG DAY

But it wasn't over yet, you had your passing off parade. All the hours spent bulling those boots and time spent on the drill square was now making sense. Then the day came, marching out showing off to your family and friends and perving on all your mates, sisters, girlfriends and the odd MILF. Finally passing off and thinking I was the dog's bollocks, until I got to my regiment. We were all as proud as punch.

At the end of it all, coming out the other side more mature and self-confident than the old me could ever have become. How the fuck did I do it. I'd finally achieved something in my life, something that many don't.

Saying goodbye to the training staff that had put me through eighteen weeks of hell was sad. I miss them all, even the biggest arseholes. Yes, there was a lot of bullying going on. Being taken round the back for a few slaps was commonplace, it happened back then, it was part of the territory not like nowadays. If you didn't pull your own weight, you got sorted out and the army had all sorts of nice ways of doing that. I, for one, had my share. I was a gobby little shit when I joined up, it soon sorted me out.

You never ever forget the lads you did your training with, the loyalty and mutual respect we had for each other. I still speak to some of them forty years later, thanks to Facebook. I wonder what happened to the rest. I'll never forget those young faces.

CIVVIES

NEIGHBOURS

We always got on with our neighbours when we were in army quarters. My neighbours never got any trouble out of me. In fact, I'd bend over backwards to do them a favour. Especially with the RSM living one side and the Provost Sergeant the other.

Now I'm out, where I live. It's completely different, you wouldn't believe the Muppets I've got living on my street.

Take my neighbour on my right, Gerald. Just the other night he was playing his 'Aga-fuckin-Doo' music loud for ages. There's only so much a man can take. If it wasn't for my missus being the voice of reason, convincing me that he was a prick and wasn't worth wasting breath over. I'd have gone around there and rammed his speakers up his arse.

Then the very next day from 0700 hours he's only knocking in nails all day, what the hell was he up to? Do they have some sort of S&M fetish going on, I thought? This went on for days, in the end I'd had enough, two can play at that game.

The missus and I decided to go away for the weekend, leaving my Edinburgh tattoo marching bands 1992 CD on repeat, with the volume at a level loud enough to really piss him off, but within the law. When I got back his missus told me, he'd had a mental breakdown, and had been admitted to hospital. She also said installation of the new floor boards will have to wait. So that's what all that banging was about.

When he came out of hospital, I had a word. I suggested he'd be wiser to go for laminated flooring otherwise he'd be getting 'THE MASSED BANDS OF THE SCOTTISH DIVISION HIGHLAND LADDIE AND THE BLACK BEAR'. My missus is away at her mum's all week, and I found my old ear defenders.

On the other side we've got this fat shy couple and I mean fat. If they were any fatter they'd go hurtling towards the sun. Anyway, the missus and I went around there on a recce one day, to introduce ourselves like good neighbours do, with a few cans of special brew.

They invited us in and we all sat in their garden, it was all very nice, he had zero sense of humour and she had a face like melted Lego. They weren't very talkative to say the least, so I thought I'd use a little military humour, you know, just as an ice breaker. Five minutes later we were back home, and I was getting the third degree from the missus.

'Why the hell did you say that? I can't take you anywhere.'
'Say what? All I said was is that why you live in a bungalow, you're both too fat to get up the stairs?'

Never seemed to hear much out of them after that. To this day I can't see anything wrong with what I said. Some people have no sense of humour. Bollocks the fucker on the other side has started banging again, where are my ear defenders?

DID YOU KNOW?

Brave Scotsman Bill Millen started playing Highland Laddie as soon as he jumped into the shallows on D-day and then walked up and down the beach playing the pipes. German prisoners later admitted that they had not attempted to shoot him because they thought he had lost his mind.

INTERACTION

When I first got out, I found it difficult to talk to and interact with most civvies,
I don't know why, but having conversations with my co-workers bored the shit out of me. I felt like saying 'I don't care what your dream was about last night or what your stupid pet cat got up to or whose claiming benefits when they're not entitled to, leave me alone and fuck off.' But I didn't, I just soldiered on.

It got that bad I even considered joining back up again, just so I could have some decent banter. Back in the military it would have been 'Will you shut the fuck up you retard, you're boring the shit out of me,' no messing.

Now I just put up with it and let them rabbit on and pretend I'm listening, dropping the occasional 'Ah' 'Yeah' and 'Mmmhh… really…'

Is it just me, am I the boring one? I decided to do a little research on the internet. Experts say small talk is good for you, if you continue to cut yourself away from small talk, you'll end up depressed as you grow older and start to moan about everything continuously. No, I bloody won't, the cheeky twats. Is that why there are so many grumpy old veterans around?

Yes, I've been out a long time now, most civvies are definitely hard bloody work. With their lack of motivation, drive, character and any sense of personal admin, I still cannot see their purpose in life, apart from paying tax of course. If they are normal, then I will happily remain a freak for the rest of my life. A grumpy old veteran. Give me ex-military any time...

CIVVY STREET TOP TIP

You are at work, it's 10am. Shout at the top of your voice 'NAAFI BREAK' ten times. Your boss will approach you and ask if you're ok. He'll then say, 'I'll tell you what, why don't you take a thirty minute break and get yourself a cup of tea.'

HEALTH AND SAFETY

The Civvies reliance on Health and Safety is laughable. 'Shit, call the duty first aider, Mandy's got a paper cut.'

'We need a meeting to form a committee and produce a manual on Paper Cut Incidents in the Workplace.' Just grab a fucking plaster for fuck's sake.

HOW TO CONFUSE THEM

When my co-workers have run out of mundane things to say like. 'I can't believe the price of bread.' I get my turn to start a conversation; it's time to get my own back. I usually start my conversation with something like…

'There I was balls deep in a camel's arse banging like a belt-fed WOMBAT when...' usually that's enough, they've started running for the exits before I can say anything else.

You might get the odd one or two civvies that might try and understand you or pretend to or jump on the bandwagon, but you can guarantee they'll be totally wide of the mark.

'Band of brothers isn't that 'The Jackson Five?'
'Shreddies isn't that a breakfast cereal?' (Definitely not for breakfast.)
'I'm off to do my Dhobi or having a Dhobi..... Civvies think I mean having a wank!

To confuse your civvy mates even more give them a few phrases and words only the military will understand. God knows what they think these mean. There are a few navy phrases in there that are interesting, even I don't know what they mean but my ex matelot son uses them. Unless he's winding me up, of course.

1. Lying like a cheap NAAFI watch.
2. Get yer wanking spanners out of yer pockets.
3. He's got more dits than a broken Morse key.
4. I've got all night, I've got a salad in the fridge and my wife is ugly.
5. What's the drill? This is warfare not welfare, slick drills quick kills.
6. Which dirty, filthy bilge rat scuppered my wet?
7. Sorry? That's what's found between shit and syphilis in the dictionary.
8. You smell like the bottom of a shit smugglers duffle bag.

9. He has more time off than Nelson's left anti flash glove.

10. The wobbly orange is chatting to the floppy sausage and the dog fuckers are playing uckers as usual!

GOING COVERT

You can always try and hide the fact that you have been in the military, but you'll have to be clever. Here are a few instant giveaways you once served.

1. When you are all called into the office for a meeting and your boss says, 'Right, let's take notes.' You pull out your notebook and HB pencil while everyone else has laptops and tablets.

2. When you go on a smoke break and you pull out your tobacco tin and make a roll up, they all stand and stare puffing away on their vapes, you say anyone want twos up?

3. When they invite you to a stag weekend in Ireland, all you can think about is the security risks and start asking for full details of the pub crawl locations, route in route out, length of stay. When, where, what?

4. You're with your workmates and you spot a fit looking bird and start shouting 'Centre of Axis pool table......'

5. When you say things like 'This office looks like the impact area at Larkhill.'

6. When you're having a heated discussion with a work college and say 'Don't answer back! I'm on

transmit you're on receive!'

Ok, some of those above will be easy to shrug off, but if you really want to blend in and pretend you're like them, here's what you should do. First of all say to yourself twenty times before work 'I am not military I am a civilian... I am not military I am a civilian... I am not military I am a civilian... A bit like Dorothy in the wizard of OZ 'There's no place like home...'

1. Forget the twenty-four hour clock. You work nine-to-five now, not 0900 to 1700 hours.

2. Stop using words like Mong, Shitter, Oolou and Gonk they will get you weird looks; it's idiot, toilet, countryside and sleep, get used to it.

3. The statement 'It's Fucked' cannot be used anymore. I know that it's hard, but the word is broken. 'It's broken,' example: this stapler is broken.

4. It's a telephone or mobile not a radio. If you're having a conversation, people need to know what you are talking about; example 'so you'll be here to give me a full brief in ten minutes, that's great, bye.' Not 'My location figures ten, for a full sit rep, roger. Out.' People will not know what you are talking about.

5. If someone annoys you that much you feel the need to give them a slap, your normal response would be 'Right, twat, I'll see you round the back of the Naafi' or in the Ring later'. Don't bother, you will be sacked on the spot and more than likely be arrested. Even McDonald's conduct background checks, and a 'conviction' for assault isn't going to help you get another job.

6. 'I was going through my shag/wank bank the other day and I remember the time I got shit faced, passed out and woke up stripped down to my boxers in a grotty council house next to a right well past-her-sell-by-date minger.' You might think it's a personal accomplishment talking about the minger that got away but your civvy work mates won't, they'll just think you're a disturbed human being!

7. And the time you knocked back twenty-five beers and pissed in your wardrobe. Reminiscing the many times you've swamped yourself is not a conversation starter.

8. Telling your workmate about the size of the turd you've just delivered in the bog will not be funny no matter how big it was, how much it hurt your arse, or how much it stank. Talking about your recent bowel movements is a definite no, no. And farting as loud as possible is "unprofessional."

9. Don't take the piss out of someone who's off sick, no matter how funny it is
telling them that any illness or injury, they have is nothing compared to the venereal diseases you contracted when you served. It won't go down well. VD is not a funny subject anymore.

10. You will upset some ladies in your office if you refer to the broken photocopier as being 'tits up' or 'cunted.'

Being able to laugh when all around you your civvy workmates have no idea what you're laughing at and how you find this funny, and then being able to laugh at the look on their face. Priceless!

To be honest I wouldn't bother trying to blend in you'll never be a civvy it's been tried before, it's impossible. Who'd want to be anyway.

DIRECTIONS

'Excuse me, could you tell me where the train station is please?'

Civvies asking veterans for directions, big mistake.

'Yes mate, you're going the wrong way, you need to about face, take a back bearing to your last known location, and re-orientate yourself, oh and don't forget your mag to grid, ETA, I'd say about figures forty I reckon, if you hurry up you'll get there before stand to.' You can just imagine the look on their face.

I THOUGHT MY DOG WAS A CIVVY

I have a dog called Pull Through, he's a Staffordshire Bull Terrier. I was convinced he was a Civvy until one afternoon when I was sitting in my conservatory and observed him. After watching him for a while I have completely changed my mind. 'That dog is definitely infantry,' I said to the missus.

I sat there in amazement when he dug shell scrape in the corner of the garden near my veggie patch on a forward slope on slightly higher ground. I couldn't have picked a better place myself, he had a brilliant field of vision and great overhead cam thanks to my cherry tree.

OUTSTANDING

Then he just sat there all day waiting, waiting for what? Even when it started to rain and his shell scrape filled with water he soldiered on. He never moved an inch. Until I shouted ENDEX out of the window, then to my amazement, he started filling in his shell scrape leaving no trace the hole was ever there and bugged out.

But the biggest give away was the next evening. He was sitting under our garden security light like he was on sentry duty when, suddenly, the light activated. In an instant, Pull Through shot off, cleared the pond, negotiated the brats climbing frame, did a right flanking and jumped our six foot wall into next door's garden with ease and cornered next door's cat. 'OUTSTANDING.' Poor pussy, it never stood a chance.

Now, as I type away on my laptop Pull Through is sitting to attention in the front room watching the England football team in the world cup on TV, howling away along with the national anthem. It makes me so proud.

Other telltale signs he's Infantry, he keeps necking my unattended glass of Herforder's when I nip off for a piss, then the other night he pissed in the wardrobe.

At first light he wakes everyone up in the street for stand to with his barking. He's also got his eye on the fat ugly Labrador bitch over the road. She's a right minger. Yes, he's definitely Infantry.

'HAVE YOU EVER KILLED ANYONE?'

Most veterans have been asked that question at least once. Why is it, civvies feel they need to know? What sort of fucked up question is that? My usual reply is; 'Yes, I've killed loads mate. Look, I got the body count tattooed on my arm.' That usually shuts them up.

Whether at work or down the pub, it's a question you should never ever ask a veteran. Especially if he or she has actually killed someone. I imagine killing someone is a deeply personal thing which can invoke exceptionally painful memories. My betting is they ask the question because they need to feed their morbid curiosity about an experience outside their own boring lives. What if that veteran has killed, does that mean he or she is a violent monster killer, what then?

I had a mate who always said 'I could never join the military. I don't think I could take someone telling me what to do all the time.' Then he joined up and got told what to do all the time. A short time later, all he kept saying was 'I can't wait to get out no one can tell me what to do anymore.' I've got news for you sunshine, almost everyone has a boss.

ARSEHOLES IN THE WORK PLACE

I find myself constantly having to watch what I say at work. My favourite saying now seems to be 'You're talking bollocks mate,' that's about as far as I go. The PC brigade is everywhere.

There are a couple of arseholes who I work with. Take Nigel for instance, his favourite saying is... 'You're not in the Army now, mate.' I feel like saying 'Thanks for reminding me you semi-literate cunt,' but I can't, I just smile and get on with it.

And then there's scruffy Duncan. Every time I see him, he's on his mobile phone or talking about who's been evicted on Big Brother or some other reality TV show, that's his life. He has no interests in anything else, what a sad existence. Please pass on my deepest condolences to your father's faulty sperm.

I would love to say to him, Duncan get off your arse,

go home and get dressed properly, you scruffy little shit and remember to switch the fucking iron on. He'd have a proper melt down. I award you fourteen days restriction of privileges. That should give you some time to consider the error of your ways. There's more to life beyond your bubble of Mobile phones and reality TV shows, Private Duncan. Turn up tomorrow morning at 06.00 hours at the Guardroom with a yellow duster and some Brasso where you'll find a lovely big cannon for you to polish. March him away, Sergeant Major. Forgive me, I got carried away with my thoughts. If only…

SHOUTING AND BAWLING

I've often wondered how the EX RSM's and drill Sergeants adapt to Civvy street, surely after spending most of their military careers shouting and bawling at anything that moves, there's no way they can stop just like that. I bet they try their hardest to control it, but it's like Tourette's, that voice gets so deeply ingrained that it can pop out at any time without you really meaning it to.

For instance, the dog isn't listening to them; 'Are you listening to me dog, what are you giving me that look for you fucking-filthy-stinking-louse-bound –flea ridden-pox infested-bastard, blah… blah… Suddenly the ex-RSM hears a child's voice. 'Have you stopped shouting now, Granddad?' They have to explain to their scared three-year-old granddaughter, hiding under the coffee table, that she can come out and they're not mad at her.

CHILLING OUT

Why do a lot of my Civvy mates including the missus, get worked up over trivial things, and stuff they can't do fuck all about, like traffic jams for instance;

'Great, yet another bloody traffic jam. It's been saying road works for the past ten bloody miles, what road works? I can't see any workers actually bloody working apart from that bloke in his cab, hold on, no, he's not, he's filling his face while reading the paper. Did you see that? They're taking the piss I'm telling you.'

Another triviality that seems drive them nuts, is delays at the airport.

'Why aren't they calling us forward? We should have taken off five minutes ago. What's the betting the in-flight meal will be cold... Look, they haven't even put our bags on yet.'

Whereas the veteran will be just chilled out with his feet up reading Bravo Two Zero or having a nap until it's time to move. Over and over again. I keep telling my missus.
'If you can do something about the problem, then do it. If you can't, then there's no point having a fucking heart attack over it.'

I suppose it's all those hurry up and wait situations sitting on the backs of vehicles in aircraft hangars, stagging on is the reason we can deal with those moments. 'Patience is counting down without blasting off.' Civvies aren't that bad really, I couldn't eat a whole one though.

WEATHER WARNING

One centimetre of snow and the UK is fucked.
February 2018 everything came to a stop again, it
happens most years. They'd been predicting it all
week, then it's, 'the snow is coming' sound the
alarms. Suddenly everyone will be joining in on that
mad dash to the supermarket, come on let's empty
the place.

But you won't find a veteran doing that, he'll just sit
there calmly waiting for the several flakes of snow to
pass. He might even pop into the garden and fire up
his barbie and wait for his civvy 'snow flake'
neighbours to return from their emergency supply live
or die run 'survival preparation for the big event'
shopping trip and ambush them with the one snow
ball he could muster from his garden.

I don't get it. Salt for the driveway, firewood, water...I
get, but not bottles of Coke, Ice creams and crisps, for
fucks sake.

Anyone who served in Germany and Canada, where
the snow is real, will know the world didn't end when
the snow fell and, boy does it fall out there. I just
shake my head at such shenanigans and laugh. All
that happened was, well, nothing really it was normal
to have a few feet of snow. Yes feet, there was no
closing of roads or schools, no news alerts and
mamby-pamby warnings to stay at home. You just
slapped your snow chains on and got on with it.

JOBS BOARD AND TIME KEEPING

When I left the military, I felt as though I was owed something, a rite of passage may be. I think it was the same for most military personnel. You find out very quickly your military skills are passed over, a lot of the time, by civilian employers. Have faith though, there are some civilian employers that really appreciate your military background. Here are a few serious suggestions.

OFFICE JOB

Why not try an office job, that's when that walking around all day with a mill board in the military trying to look busy till knocking off time comes in handy. But this time you can do that sitting on your arse. Basically, spending most of the day browsing eBay, YouTube and on the rare occasion somebody approaches your desk you flick to your work stuff. Be warned though, you might actually have to do some work now and then. The pay's not bad, at least £20 to £30 grand a year and that's just from your eBay shop.

HITMAN

You could become a hitman. After all, that's what most of us were in the military anyway! I wouldn't take up too big a contract straight away like taking out the US president, for instance, he has two-hundred bodyguards, far too much protection. I'd recommend you do a practice run to see if you've got the bottle. Go for someone a bit more low profile like that Mr Upton the PE teacher that touched your arse all those years ago. He has no such protection and is a much easier beginner's target.

**MR UPTON
THE PE
TEACHER**

SAFARI GUIDE

Why not go to university for a few years, study hard
and gain a Zoology degree, that with the skills you
gained in the military, could get you a job as a safari
guide on a game reserve in Africa. But remember
there are serious differences between A. Lions and B.
Bunny rabbits.

FOOTBALL MANAGER

What about becoming a football Manager, it's a bit cut
throat, but with those man management skills that
were drilled into you in the military, I'm sure they'll
help you to get to the end of the season. And if you
manage to perform well enough, you might secure yet
another lucrative contract, before your missus comes
home from work, switches off your computer game
and asks you whether you've been down the Job

Centre today, and you reply 'No, but I've just bought Harry Kane for fifty million, what a fucking bargain.'

TIME KEEPING

Let's face it, you never really slept in the military. You slept but you still knew what was going on around you. On deployment or on exercise, there was always some clumsy bastard that would tread on you in your gonk bag in the dark.

Back in your accommodation, getting a torch shone in your face by the guard in the middle of the night looking for somebody that hadn't booked in, it was a regular occurrence. 'Sorry mate, wrong pit' or someone would come back off the piss and insist you were going to help them eat their kebab before they pissed in your locker during the night. Before you knew it, it was Wakey-Wakey, rise and shine, hands off cocks on with socks.

All ex-military know the saying 'if you're on time, you're late.' It was drilled into us that we had to be fully dressed and out through the door quicker than you can say 'Get outside now before you get my size ten implanted in your arse. MOVE IT.' Depending what rank you were, obviously.

This was first developed in basic training and, then, perfected over our years of service. We also found ourselves waking up twenty-minutes earlier than we needed to. To make sure we were ready for any eventuality. Never late and always arrive on time.

A lot different to what I have to put up with now that I'm out. Some of these Civvies attitudes to time keeping fucking stinks. I don't know about you, but even after being out all these years, lateness irritates the crap out of me.

It's not just lateness. When it comes to finishing time, after they've been pretending to work all day, regardless of what's going on at 5pm, they are out of there in a flash in their cars and off for their daily dose of road rage sitting in traffic jams. I can't do that, I leave when the job is done!

Sometime after I left the military, I decided to get a job as a static security officer. I arrived at work on my first day thirty minutes before my twelve-hour shift started, like you do. I've nearly completed my shift and you've guessed it, no fucker turns up to take me off.

No phone call, nothing, I gave it ten minutes, still nothing. So now I'm on the phone to control to ask them if I was going to get relieved anytime today. They said we'll phone him to see where he is. Fair enough, shit happens, I thought. Another ten minutes pass so I call again. Yes, we're sorry about that, we've been phoning and phoning him, he's not answering his phone. We think he might have overlaid, so we've sent a mobile patrol vehicle to his house to wake him up.

The mobile patrol vehicle is heading for Burton from Sheffield, I work in Derby. I'm totally pissed off. Two hours later, this scruffy twat turns up saying... 'Sorry I'm late, I only had a few hours' sleep last night. I didn't get in from the pub until two o'clock.' Is this bloke taking the piss, does he really think that's a credible excuse? I bit my lip, I didn't say a word and went home. The next day, more of the same, he was late again this time the traffic was bad. What at 06.00 hours in the morning?

On the fourth morning he couldn't come in he'd gone sick with stress and a sore arse, where I'd implanted my size twelve boot up it. I went home to explain to the missus why I didn't have a job anymore. 'You can't do that out here, this is CIVVY STREET' she said.

Honestly, some of the most fucked up excuses I've heard for being late for work, the dog ate my alarm clock, I've just bought a solar powered scooter when suddenly it started raining and it just stopped, I was being followed so I took a longer route. What next? I was kidnapped by aliens... my cat had fucking hiccups.

I know one thing you'll be hard-pressed to find a veteran who is willingly late to anything. It would eat into us, stress us out, the thought of letting your oppo, buddy down would give us a migraine. Timing is everything. If you're early you're on time, if you're on time you're late and if you're late, you're fucked.

DRINKING

Those crazy drinking sessions in the military, when you were shitfaced before nine o'clock and you drank your own body weight in beer, this happened quite often in Germany where beer was cheap. Those sessions are all but memories now. There are still occasions when I re-visit the past and head out for a night on the town, or a friend's stag night, or when I meet up with a few army buddies for a proper Military/veteran beer drinking binge night.

Apart from my BAOR days, I've never been much of a beer drinker, but I do compromise and drink pretty much everything else behind the bar. On the rare occasion I do drink beer, I have to pace myself. Some of my ex-army mates can drink ten beers plus, no problem.

What constitutes a proper Military/veteran beer drinking binge? Ten pints... eleven pints? Where are you on the veterans drinking chart?

THE VETERANS DRINKING CHART

Zero Beers – Sober. The non-drinker. 'Sorry I don't drink, never did, never will.' (Never trust a man that doesn't drink!) That's what they say. The non-drinker is always useful if he sticks around. He's your taxi home, the one that stops you from making a twat of yourself, like starting on bouncers when you've had too many, doing Moonies or taking your clothes off and jumping in fountains, you know those 'watch this everyone' stunts. The non-drinker will be the one sitting in A&E with you until 4am.

One Beer - Feeling happy. 'Right, that's me done, got to get home I'm driving. Anybody else want a lift? No, just me then, I'll see you at work in the morning.' Always rattles his keys, pretends he's one of the lads usually a civvy. Good for buying the first round, feels guilty. The one beer man is probably under the thumb.

Second Beer - On your way. Right, that's the let downs got rid of. Start getting cravings for pork scratching and scampi fries. The second beer always goes down quickly. 'Come on lads drink up, we're slacking.' Then the friendly argument begins about who's going to buy the next round. 'I'll get it,' 'No, you put your money away, I'll get this one.' 'Too late lads I've got them in.' The second beer man sometimes slips away undetected. He's either pulled or remembered the football is on live next door.

Third Beer - Tipsy, slight memory loss. It's, pull up a sand bag time, laughing loudly at funny exaggerated war stories from back in the dark ages. Uses cheesy chat up lines. Pleasure senses are now activated, compliment the barmaid on her choice of blouse. The third beer man by now desperately needs to visit the bog, the seal is broken. On his way there, tries his hardest to let everyone know he's sober by the way he walks, it worked this time. By the time he reappears everyone else has moved on.

Fourth Beer - Chemically imbalanced. Blood alcohol levels begin to peak reducing your brain capacity, which causes you to start talking shit. 'Eh, let's get a tattoo?' Who wants an arm wrestle? Start making future plans, Night club, going for a curry. Fourth beer man wants to go home, but he's got no chance his buddies won't let him.

Fifth Beer - Well oiled. Starting to spill your beer, slurred speech, mapping out the rest of your life on a beer mat. Everyone is drunk and pretends they're listening. This is where I make an excuse and head for the last bus or get a lift off Zero beer, if he's still around. 'Sorry lads got to go the cat's not well and the missus is worried.' 'Clive your cat died remember, you used that excuse last time.' There's no escape.

Sixth Beer – Trashed. Some double vision, slurring and wobbling around. Head for your second piss, trying to pretend you are sober. Makes it, just. The sixth beer man is using his head against the urinal wall to steady himself, long piss, telling himself he's capable of making his way back to his buddies without assistance...Come on you can do this. You can do this.

Seventh Beer – Steaming. Talking absolute bollocks. Sends drink over to the woman sitting at the opposite table. No reaction. Her boyfriend asks you outside, you buy him a drink too! The seventh beer man will start to raise his voice and sing along with the piped music, every song is the best song ever and is a karaoke song.

Eighth Beer – Bladdered. Fall over, get up, fall over. Offer to buy drinks for everyone in the room. Lots of people say yes. The eighth beer man will go around the bar hugging everyone. Fall over. Get up. Say 'You're my best mate, you are' to people you've just met. Tell your mates you're going to do the dance of the flamers. The ex-military landlord says, 'No you're fucking not.'

Ninth Beer – Hammered. Head-ache kicks in. Want to show everyone you can take your beer and drink it down in five seconds, spill most of it, put the glass on your head. That boyfriend from earlier asks you outside again, all your veteran mates get up. He walks away. Decide to go to another pub. The ninth beer man is fighting nausea on the way but makes it.

Tenth Beer – Plastered. In the bog being sick. Come out to try and play on the fruit machine with blurred vision, don't know what you're doing. Start to shout at the machine. Stand on the table shouting abuse at all four bartenders, pull a Moonie, where's Zero beer? He went home ages ago. Fall off the table, it's time to head home, tenth beer man.

Eleventh Beer Plus - You're out of your face. Speech no longer possible. Everyone manages to find the exit apart from you. You're back in the pub toilets wondering how you get out the place, passed out, man down, rescued by one of your veteran buddies (Never leave a man behind.)

Night Club – Cunted. Complete zombie, waiting patiently in the freezing cold to get into the overpriced nightclub, there's pushing and shoving, you are trying your hardest to look in control well behaved, when you eventually get to the door, the bouncers say;

'Sorry mate, you're not coming in here.'
'Come on mate be fair, is it because I can't walk?'
'No, it's because moving up the queue on your hands and knees, is a bit of a giveaway… On your bike.'

Take on The World – Legless. Brave, upset, start to abuse the 6'5 bouncer. Get dragged away by your mates. Keep saying 'what are you looking at, leave me alone, I could have him.' Decline a taxi with your mates, you can't be arsed to wait. Decide to walk home, even though it's five miles away. Your Kebab compass is not making sense.

Taxi - Rat-arsed. Doing a back bearing on kebab compass, arrive back at the taxi rank, now wearing a Police bollard, soaking wet after falling in the fountain. Put in a cab by somebody, the taxi driver is paid and given your home address and you're taken home. Generally pleased at the way the evening has gone while trying your hardest not to throw up in the back of the taxi.

Home! - Shit-faced. You can't get the key in the door. Then you realize the bastards have given the taxi driver the address of your local dentist. Bastards, it must have been that one matelot mate. Feeling ill, trying to stop the world from spinning, passed out flat on your back. A passerby, who knows you, thinks you're dead and nearly calls an ambulance. 'Come on mate, what are you doing down there?' 'I'm showing God what I look like standing up. Who the fuck are you?'

Home Safely – Wankered. Missus finds you asleep on your doorstep and drags you inside. A little while later in your living room, there you are trousers around ankles, waste paper bin on your head, watching roulette on the TV, consciously awake, but physically in a coma. You have no idea how you ended up at home. You want to order an Indian you'll never eat, but your missus is one step ahead and has hidden your phone.

The next day, your head feels like a bag of smashed arseholes. Never again, you've decided to go dry again, leave drinking to the experts. The missus agrees. Now you have to explain the love bites on your neck.

THE DARK SIDE

I covered this in ENDEX 1, but I feel it deserves to be mentioned again. GB, Australia, Canada, New Zealand, South Africa and the US, it doesn't matter what country you served, military across the world share the same humour, a special kind of humour. Apart from the Germans, they have no sense of humour. Only joking, Fritz!

The same can be said for those who work in the emergency services too. Fireman/Police/A&E staff/paramedic's they just have their own version. In fact, I've been told Ambulance crews sense of humour is so dark you need to put a fucking light on!

It's all about the ability to laugh in the direst of circumstances and still function. It goes a long way to get you through a difficult moment. The only people who see us all as sick fucks for what we joke about, are the people who don't understand why we do it. They've probably never experienced what we've been through and seen, some of us on a daily basis.

Laughing and joking about situations that really deserve huge amounts of sympathy. It's a military thing, the ability to take the piss out of a shit situation. Patrolling the streets of Belfast, eyes scanning everywhere, you could never switch off, if you did, you could guarantee something would happen and it did to me.

We were patrolling down Clonard Street, just off the Falls Road, when I got hit in the back of the head by a missile. I think it was a large stone or a lump of metal, probably fired from a catapult. The impact knocked me clean off my feet. The next minute I was out cold. Coming round minutes later, I remember an RUC Officer standing over me showing me his twisted deformed finger saying 'you'll be alright there sonny, I got £500 for a broken finger.'

Every fucker started to laugh apart from me. For the next few weeks, after coming out of the hospital, then walking round North Howard Street Mill on light duty's. Everyone took the piss. The back of my head was shaved, which revealed a massive lump with a scab on it, resembling a massive zit. 'You see Wardi, you're that thick nothing can penetrate that skull of yours', I kept being told. Fuck me, I'd been injured in Belfast. I wanted sympathy… no chance of that.

When I arrived back from Belfast a few months later, I received £750 Criminal Injuries Compensation. The Irish copper was right! It was my turn to laugh now.

Lack of sympathy could come in all shapes and forms, some of which could be brutal. I read somewhere about a lad in one of the Scottish regiments who had a brain tumour. After emergency surgery, they put a metal plate in his skull. After months of R&R, on his first day back at his unit he was greeted with 'You're back then 'Robo-jock!'

In the military they don't say 'it's ok, it didn't work, relax, take a deep breath and try again' they say, 'are you a fucking retard or something?'

An old veteran is sitting on a park bench, a young lad with spiked hair that is all different colours, green, red, orange, blue and yellow walks up and sits down next to him. The veteran just stares.

The young man says. 'What's the matter with you? Never done anything wild in your life?'
The veteran replies, 'Got drunk once and fucked with a parrot. I was just wondering if you were my son.'

Two old vets sat on the bus.

'Have you heard? Old Ted's dead.'
'Yes, I heard that, very sad. What was it?'
'Oh, nothing serious.'

At a social function a soldier got talking to a lady in her late 40s.

Lady - 'This is the first time I have been out since I lost my husband to cancer two years ago'
Squaddie - 'Sorry to hear that, this is your first time out socially, then?'
Lady – 'Yes' answers the poor widow lady.
Squaddie - 'God… You must be fucking gagging for it then.'

Being ex-military, you have a distinctive way of greeting people.

You see a mate you haven't seen for years and you

start the conservation with...

'Oi wanker!!!!!!!'
'Oh, it's you, you arse wipe, where've you been cunty bollocks?'

Or

'Morning twat'
'Fuck off knob jockey 'or 'cockwomble.'

Civvies would have a fit, if you spoke to them like that. Those are just normal greetings to us. Abusive banter is a military thing.

You enter a pub. You buy your drink and sit down, there's a guy sitting next to you, how can you be sure he's a veteran? He'll be sarcastic and say... 'I'm glad you're here. I should have been taken off stag half an hour ago, you wanker.'

THE CRACK, WIND UP, PRANK
Having a laugh at someone else's expense is something that helps you to cope in certain situations. As we know, this happened on a daily basis, usually when boredom set in. Whether in the mess or in the barrack room, when it strikes it can get really sick.

My son, he's ex-Navy, told me they used to get up to some right disgusting stuff like wank into an oppo's socks and put them back in his shoes. Then lay there in their racks waiting for the oppo to put them on. Then start laughing that hard they hurt themselves, and their oppo is also laughing that hard he is physically incapable of helping them. I'm sure everybody's been there. Civvies would say 'that's not funny.' I suppose it isn't to them. Ever since he told me, I always check my socks.

Sleeping naked on top of your pit was a big mistake, all I'm saying is pubic hair burns really well. Like dead grass, one spark will turn your nether regions into a towering inferno, like one of those inflame Spanish ships escaping from the Armada. You disappear into the bogs to put it out.

Let's face it you don't go down your local and see someone starkers on the bar doing the Dance of the Flamers, do you? All we are doing is making fun of ourselves, laughing at ourselves, making the time pass quicker. We get it, but most civilians never will.

We all know it can get much worse. God knows what they'd think of someone – warning! Don't read on snowflakes, if easily offended - drinking their own piss, or drinking somebody else's piss, for a bet. I wonder if this sort of thing still goes on in today's military, I bet it does.

Taking photos of your turds to show to your mates. Humping a tin of compo sausages, which I'll come to later… Having the crack, taking the piss, telling the sick joke, it's all part of military life. If you're not taking the piss out of someone, then you probably don't like them. Still being mates with people who have punched you whilst drunk, all comes with the territory. But I suppose the buck has to stop somewhere… Like fuck it does!

**Compo,
Food of the Gods**

Here are a few memories from long ago for the old and bold compo commandos. The twenty-four hour, four-man and ten-man ration packs from the 60's, 70s and 80s, although the menus were always being updated, it is said that they were the best. But you may disagree.

From the mid 1970's the basic ration pack was, the 'twenty-four hour ration pack GS (General Service). This contained enough calories to sustain a man in the field for one day and was available in four different menus. Heximin Cooker & Tablets were issued separately.

Four and ten-man ration packs - mainly standard tins - were intended for central feeding. Biscuits or bread was issued separately, along with fresh vegetables if available. The Heximin Cooker & Tablets were also issued, if requested. They were designed to last for up to three years in any climate.

We didn't know how lucky we were back then... Steak and Onion, Stewed Steak, Steak and kidney pudding, Chicken Supreme, Chicken Curry, Salmon, Corned Beef, Bacon Grill, bacon burgers, sausages, baked beans, peas, cheese possessed, raspberry and plum jam in a tube, rice pudding, custard, ginger pudding, spotted dick, fruitcake, oatmeal blocks, mixed veg, carrots, potato powder, tinned pears, peaches, mixed fruit cocktail. Spangles, Tiffin chocolate bars, boiled sweets, dextrose tablets, dried soup, including Mulligatawny, Mock turtle, Oxtail, Chicken, Mushroom, Tomato, and Goulash - condemned and listed under crimes against humanity - and replaced with Irish stew and lots more.

There were various menus, but I always seemed to end up with the same one, for some reason. When you were on foot you were nearly always issued with twenty-four hour ration packs, sometimes we were issued with four man or the ten man ration packs to split down. They weighed a ton to cart about. Sometimes you had to sacrifice other bits of kit to fit it all in. At the end of the day, what would you rather carry a belt of fifty blank or a can of compo sausages. No brainier, unless you were lucky enough to have an APC, tank or vehicle to sling it all in.

Remember those mornings freezing your nuts off in a German wood on exercise. You've just had a wash using your mess tin in sub-zero temperatures, while in your other mess tin your-all-in-one breakfast is frying away, 1x sausage, a slice bacon grill, beans and, if you were lucky, an egg that has survived so far. Not forgetting the "extras" grass, gravel, engine oil, gun oil, etc. All served up on a stale 'it'll do' slice of white RAOC bread with added black fingerprints and the sprinkled ash from a part-burnt fag, all washed down with a hot 'forestry block flavoured' brew in your black mug.

BLACK MUG

No one is in any doubt that compo had its side effects. You could guarantee by day three of living on the stuff, you'd be bunged up for at least a week or more. Rumour has it the ration packs were designed to do exactly that.

On the seventh day after trying and failing to have a dump all day that night all hell would break loose. It usually happened during the 0200-0400 stag. It felt like the world had just fallen out of your arse.

Right own up. 'Whose is that?' came the cry at first light when some poor fucker had just discovered a massive foot long Richard the third in some poor fucker's trench, that had been mistaken for the shit pit when someone got lost in the wood.

Let's be honest here, having a dump in the woods after days of compo.... Holding onto your shovel for support with one hand, smoking a ciggy with the other. The sheer joy and relief was orgasmic, it was your moment. For five minutes you were the happiest bloke on exercise! Sometimes, though, you couldn't just leave it there. People needed to see it, witness it. This fucker belonged in the Guinness book of records.

I thought the Compo of my day late 60's to 90's was spot on. I have no idea what the troops in the field are fed on today. I know one thing the new rations, no longer have the same luxuries that we once enjoyed. I heard it's that bag crap now. I say bring back the compo sausage.

Maybe in thirty or forty years' time those currently in the military will be looking back on their rations like we do now, and like they did after WW1 & WW2. Here's some of the stuff we used to live on back in the day in detail. I've given them an Endex rating of zero to 10. Zero=WMD.

Oh, and one more thing, did anyone ever actually use the range cards printed on the twenty-four hour ration packs? If you did, you're one sad individual.

PILCHARDS AND SARDINES

There were a few brave souls that tackled those and lived to tell the story, some didn't make it. Usually they were dealt with straight away using High Explosives or buried. I'd hate to think how many tins there are buried in war zones and training areas around the world. Isn't it funny you don't hear of wild boar in Germany anymore. It's because they took a liking to compo pilchards they'd uncovered while rummaging in the undergrowth.

ENDEX RATING... WMD

WILD BOAR

SAUSAGES

For me the best thing that came out of the cold war was compo sausages, putty in a tin. Also known as ET fingers, or dead man's fingers. These sausages were usually found in the four or ten-man ration packs. What would I give for a can of these right now. Perhaps the finest culinary delight the ration packs had to offer. I've seen grown men fight over the last COMPO sausage at breakfast. There were ten sausages in a tin. You can be sure if there was ever an odd one left it would be cut and shared to the millimetre. I remember being served up breakfast in the field one morning, usually it would be one egg, beans, slice of bacon grill and one sausage. But on this occasion, I was lucky I got an extra sausage due to one of the cooks being my drinking buddy. Arriving back to my section with two sausages caused a deadly silence, if looks could kill. I got it down my neck quickly before I was mugged.

When on the rare occasion we managed to get a whole tin to ourselves, we'd pierce the top, slap it around the Land Rover manifold, with all that fat packed sizzling around them, fifteen minutes later hot delicious sausages. Mind you, I haven't a clue what was in them though, I know it wasn't meat that's for sure. I think it would it be safer not to ask.

ENDEX RATING... 10

DID YOU KNOW?

Barkers was the trench slang for sausages issued by the Army in WW1. This was coined because the soldiers believed the sausages contained dog meat. Nothing changes then!

ACC URBAN LEGEND

In the world of compo, the sausage sex aid may be king. Rumour has it for a spot of field loving, if you removed the middle sausage from the tin it would provide you with an excellent artificial vagina. Never tried it myself, honest. Shagging tins of sausages... There's a recipe for trouble. Here's me thinking that thick white goo was fat. Warning it carries 56 days jankers if caught. All I can say is they must have had small willies. I wonder if any ex-ACC screams 'One fucking sausage!' in his sleep... Like my missus does.

BACON GRILL

The second best thing to come out the cold war. Just cut it into slices and fry, or if there was no time to cook it, and there usually wasn't, it was great eaten cold on the move. I can remember when I had my first fried Bacon Grill... I had it with a fresh egg nicked from some Herman, the German's farm.

ENDEX RATING... 8

BACON BURGERS

Dogs go wild and start to howl for miles around when you open a can of this stuff. When eaten cold it would give you instant heartburn, and a horrible chalky, orange lardy after taste in the roof of your mouth for days. Rumour has it, it's made from Sweeny Todd's leftovers. Warning if you wanted to waste a few hours of your life, don't try frying Bacon burgers and Bacon grill in your mess tin. It took forever to clean them. It was that bad there were some that would give up and throw their mess tins away.

ENDEX RATING... 6

STEAK AND KIDNEY PUDDING

Snake and Sydney Pudding – also known as Babies' heads. Food of the gods probably, if cooked properly. Another one that is up there with best. Called babies' heads because they looked like them when they came slithering out of the can. Seriously I couldn't tell you what the meat was, but it tasted great with smash. Just dent the tin and boil it up in your mess tin for about 15 minutes, then open it with your thumb breaker compo tin opener. I used to love watching sprogs end up with a face full of hot boiling fat squirting into the eyes when they pierced the tin.

ENDEX RATING... 9

MESS TINS

BISCUITS AB

Meaning *Alternative Bread* or *Anal Blockage*. One word, indestructible! There was always a rumour going around that they were used in early body-armour testing for ballistic resistance. They were also a handy digging tool. You had to be seriously hungry to eat them on their own. They had to be accompanied with something. Jam, cheese possessed or condensed milk. Biscuits AB is the reason I have no teeth now. They should have been called ABH biscuits. I think they're still around, nowadays they call them biscuits Brown.

I haven't got a clue what they were made of, back then. After chatting to an Ex-army slop jockey, who I can't name, he gave me what is thought to be the top secret ingredients; 500mg bromide, 300mg cement, 250 mg sand and 2 spoons of gunpowder mixed with Swarfega, then cook at 550 C for 36 hours. That was a reason why they were known as the Aldershot Concrete Company.

ENDEX RATING... WMD

BISCUITS AB FRUIT

Dead fly biscuits, also known as Garibaldi biscuits. When I took them home to my army quarter me and the missus used to tell the brats they had dead flies in them, so we could hog them all to ourselves.

In the factory where they're made what's the betting the workers throw in the odd dead fly. I would.

ENDEX RATING... 6

OATMEAL BLOCKS

The crème de la crème, the Oatmeal Blocks with their high sugar content, they were something else. Whether you're making a satisfying porridge when mixed with condensed milk and hot water, or just munching on one whilst lost on patrol, they were perfect.

There were never enough of them to go around. They were the cause of many an argument if not shared fairly. Don't fucking mess with another man's Oatmeal, I've seen soldiers fight to the death for those. There are lots of Civvy imitations in the shops, but you'll never beat the original.

ENDEX RATING... 10

DID YOU KNOW?

Back in the day, once a box of compo had reached its Eat by Date, it would be sent off to be tested, if it passed it would have its life extended.

THE TOILET PAPER

Where do I start? I don't know why they bothered, 2 sheets was never enough. I think because they knew they'd bunged us up for a week. 7 x 2 =14 sheets, seven days worth would be enough. It wasn't. Made of grease-proof paper, I seem to remember it had Government Property printed on every sheet. Why, for fuck's sake? Were they worried someone would nick it? They shouldn't have bothered all it was good for was tracing paper for my brats or for making roll ups when you ran out of rizlas.

ENDEX RATING... 1

TUBES

Tooth paste like tubes of condensed milk which resembled sperm. You only got these in the one-man, twenty-four hour packs. Cum cream, as we used to call it, great for wind ups, like emptying half a tube in someone's sleeping bag. There were other tubes containing black-currant, raspberry, gooseberry or damson jam, great for sucking on when tabbing.

ENDEX RATING... 7

MOCK TURTLE SOUP

Disgusting stuff, what the fuck was it? Was it supposed to mock the taste of an actual turtle? After doing a little research what they didn't tell you is that it was actually made from sheep's brains, internal organs and other nasties like calf's head or foot, so it duplicated the taste of turtle meat. Sheep's brains? That explains a lot! It is also believed the MOD took a packet of the soup for chemical warfare trials, it failed, and was banned because it was too lethal.

ENDEX RATING... WMD

DID YOU KNOW?

In Aden in '61 they had ration packs containing tins of cigarettes and self-heating tins of soup. It had a small firework at the base with a ring pull. I wonder if they ever got them mixed up with grenades that would be funny. After throwing the grenade and hitting the deck, instead of shouting grenade, you shout chicken and mushroom or words to that effect.

PROSSESSED CHEESE 'CHEESE POSSESSED'

Cheese anti-tank! Good for fixing your boot soles and radiator leaks. Poke a piece of string down through the centre and you have a candle. You can even eat it, if you are brave enough.

In the 70's the jungle natives of Belize would risk their lives running along the road, trying to catch a discarded can of compo cheese and other compo delights, which travelled at 15 mph from the back of a departing 4 tonner, full of troops on their way out of the jungle after training. Sadly, they were wiped out not long after that. Must be something they ate.

This stuff was indestructible. I heard it had reputedly been fired down the range by Chieftain Tanks. It even refused to burn or melt, no matter what you did to it. I bet if you launched it towards the sun it wouldn't melt. And lastly, it was against the Geneva Convention to feed it to POW's.

ENDEX RATING... 4

TOP TIP

Cheese possessed is good for removing stubborn permanent marker ink from maps. Also makes great fishing bait. As soon as you open a can on the river bank the fish start jumping out of the water.

CHICKEN SUPREME

Proof that Satan exists. It was like eating newspaper in wallpaper paste. I couldn't stomach the stuff. The missus didn't agree she loved the stuff. She managed to wallpaper the whole army quarter with just 6 tins.

ENDEX RATING... 5 (BECAUSE THE MISSUS LIKED IT)

CHOCOLATE AND BOILED SWEETS

The tins of 5 Tiffin bars and boiled sweets were highly prized items. Turn your back for one minute and the tin would vanish. In the four-man packs there was always arguing over the fifth bar of chocolate.

ENDEX RATING... 8

ROLLO'S

The good old British Rollo, or were they? I remember the one's in the ration packs having Arabic writing on the wrapping. They didn't taste like your standard Rollo, they had that white been stored in a warm-place look about them. Obviously sold to the Saudi's left to rot in some fucking camel shed, re-packaged then sold back to us. The MOD must have done some dodgy deals back in the day. Some sort of weapons for Rollo's deal that backfired. 'Ere those missiles you sold us were crap have your fucking Rollo's back.

I remember grabbing my shovel and two sheets of compo issued toilet paper and disappearing into the forestry block and returning minutes later with a scrunched up whole packet of Rollo's on my shovel and saying to my trench buddy 'look at the size of that bastard' then flinging it at him. Childish, I know, but let's face it, we were all brats back then.

ENDEX RATING... 4

AZTEC BAR

Remember the Aztec bar? It was considered a treat to get the packs that contained them. It was a bit like an imitation Mars bar, but with raisins and a hint of rum. Probably another failed high street chocolate bar the military bought up for peanuts. You always knew when the compo was Old & Out of date. You still found Aztec bars in them! (If you were born in the 80's you won't have a clue what I'm jabbering on about.)

ENDEX RATING... 4

SPANGLES

You could never get the wrappers off, they were always welded together. I remember hours of sitting on the side of my trench trying to prise the fuckers apart without the wrapping paper attached to it, wearing my NBC gloves. Red ones were best though.

They say the smell from the strawberry flavoured spangle was that strong, it would give your position away from 300 yards or a mile in the jungle.

ENDEX RATING... 7

DEXTROSE TABLETS

It is said they were put in the compo rations to provide you with extra energy to get to your destination quicker, the fucking bog! They made great laxatives.

ENDEX RATING...5

MIXED FRUIT PUDDING

It didn't really do anything for me. It was always the last tin in the box along with the margarine; it did have its uses though. Again, great for making those childish fake turds out of and leaving them in people's boots just before they were woken up to stag on.

ENDEX RATING... 3

THE HEXI COOKER & BLOCKS

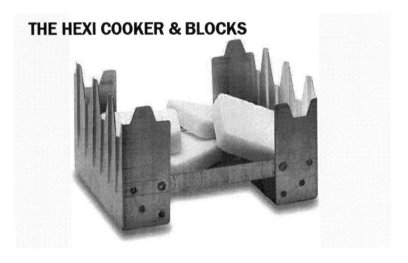

They were a throwaway item. If you ever got to the point where you actually cooked something with it, you were lucky. Fill your mess tin with water, pop in your tin of whatever and boil away. Once cooked, use the rest of the water for a brew if you got that far. Nine times out of ten you heard the call, prepare to fucking move, stand to or gas, gas, gas, so the whole exercise was a waste of time. And your Hexi cooker was too hot to put away, unless you wanted to melt your green gloves.

ENDEX RATING... 7

CAN DISPOSAL

On exercise the empty cans were usually crushed and buried in the bottom of your trench. Or, when no one was around, shoved down the exhaust pipe of your 432 and propelled into the forestry block. But we never did that!

PAD BOUND

Any leftovers would always end up being pad bound. It was a sort of food bank, especially at the end of the month. I remember when I was in Germany, arriving home from exercise a number of times carrying my large black bin-liner full of compo.
The brats thought it was Christmas day morning fighting on the floor for that 5th Tiffin bar and trying to get the paper off the spangles. Then at night once the brats were in bed sucking on their tubes of condensed milk, the missus and I would tuck into a romantic welcome home three course meal, menu A of course.

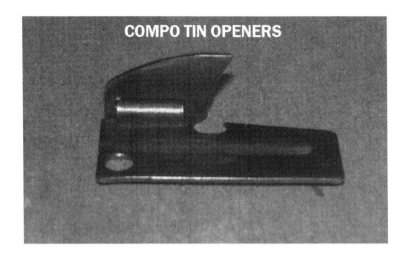

COMPO TIN OPENERS

Last but not least, what about those magic indestructible compo tin openers? I've still got a few in my KFS drawer years later, and they still work. Much better than these fancy civvy can openers, these things last forever. A front-line Infantry soldier's life expectancy in battle against a red army attack is nine seconds. Compo tin openers is 39 years.

FIELD KITCHENS

When in the field, it was compo every day. Sometimes the slop jockeys came out into the field with their field kitchens, bringing with them fresh rations, although most of what they gave us was still compo. Then we'd head back to camp, if you lived in you'd be looking forward to a fresh proper meal. Except, sometimes we were told we hadn't eaten enough Compo and we had to reduce the stockpile. We'd end up living on compo for another few weeks.

FACT

All in all, Compo back then was good stuff. It was a lot better than what the red army got, I'm sure. I bet theirs hadn't changed since Stalingrad. Compo did its job, it kept the troops moving and guaranteed to seal your lower intestine shut for at least a week. What's the betting the MoD still has an aircraft hangar full of the old retro compo in some remote part of the country......'Just in case'...... Like they drag out the green goddesses in times of crisis, watch out Britain.

Now and again, you see the odd can of compo appear on eBay for some ridiculous price. My advice is to get in the loft or the garage and start digging down into the bottom of your old Bergen. You might find that long lost tin of oatmeal blocks or bacon grill or, if you're really lucky, the artificial vagina. Don't stay up there too long, the missus will know what you're up to if she reads this book.

Today's twenty-four hour ration packs are mostly boil in the bag crap. They are not as good as the old stuff but, at least, it can easily be packed away in their kit or pouches, not like the old tinned stuff. I know what I'd rather have.

ROAD RAGE AND SALESMEN

You're driving down the dual carriage minding your own business on the outside lane abiding by the speed limit. All of a sudden, a GET-OUT-OF-MY-FUCKING-WAY BMW appears out of nowhere. It drives up behind you, thinking he has a built in right of way device fitted to his souped up, tinted window, private reg (TWAT 1) car. The driver has obviously gotten an 'I've got more money than you' attitude and thinks that entitles him to get to his destination one second before you do. The normal, sensible, responsible driver would just let him pass, he gets it he's going faster.

Alternatively, the crazy, oh-you-want-a-race-do-you? type of person would lose it and zoom off into the distance. Now it's the Monaco grand prix. But this time he's met his match he's tailgating a veteran.

Your veteran on the other hand can't be bothered with all that drama. A veteran has identified the car driver behind him is an arsehole and will just maintain his current speed or might even slow down a little, with the attitude 'NO ONE WILL PASS.' Here's how it goes…

STAGE 1

Actions on: The BMW is now flashing his main beam at you.

Veteran: Find a nice slow lorry on the inside lane and adopt the NO ONE WILL PASS Sunday driver mode.

STAGE 2

Actions on: Now the BMW is doing some serious tailgating and giving you the WANKER sign out the window.
Veteran: Windscreen washer on, 5-10 second bursts plus rear fog lights forcing him to drop back.

STAGE 3

Actions on: It looks like he's come to his senses and pulls back
Veteran: you're not fooled, keeping a close eye on BMW, indicate to enter the inside lane and let him pass.

STAGE 4

Actions on: He sees his chance the old cunt has given up! He puts his foot down preparing to give you the V sign on his way past.
Veteran: You've changed your mind and safely indicate moving back into the outside lane. Finding an even slower lorry on the inside lane.

STAGE 5

Action on: The BMW is waiting to pounce, he won't be beaten as you both approach the traffic lights
Veteran: lights are green. Slow right down and time it just right so they start to change, speed up and go through legally (just).

STAGE 6

Action on: BMW goes through on red
Veteran: You drive away smiling while the twat behind you is pulled.

STAGE 7

Action on: The missus makes an observation 'You're a bloody idiot, are you trying to get me killed, every time you take me shopping this happens....'
Veteran: Turn music up, the rabbit song by Chaz and Dave.

12 THINGS DRIVERS HATE ABOUT OTHER DRIVERS

1. People who pick their noses at traffic lights
2. Twats who drive with the front fogs on, on a sunny day
3. Middle lane drivers
4. 4x4's that do the school run and have never seen mud
5. Getting cut up by white van man
6. Drivers changing lanes without looking.
7. Foreign drivers going around roundabouts the wrong way
8. The local cycling club's out for the day holding up the traffic by riding 12 deep & 5 abreast!
9. Sneaky coppers
10. Twats trying to negotiate their shitty 900cc Fiat through a gap you could fit a Challenger tank through.
11. Sunday drivers
12. People that put dozens of crap tree car air fresheners around their rear-view mirror.

ROAD SIGNS

SUICIDAL DEER

OFFICERS MAP READING

RAF BASE

SENNYBRIDGE

RMP DISPLAY TEAM

SUGAR DADDY

PULL UP A SAND BAG

NATO STANDARD

DIGGING IN

SALESMEN

Everybody hates them, especially veterans. It's not just the people who knock on my door trying to sell religion, no thanks, I don't want to hear about how you can save me from eternal damnation, they're easily gotten rid of. I just say. 'I'm having a black mass down my cellar, you're quite welcome to join us if you want'. They usually just smile and go away. It's the door to door salesmen I hate most, the ones that won't take no for an answer.

The dignified way of getting rid of them is by saying. 'No offence mate, but I won't be buying today' after all they're only trying to make a living. Veterans can't do that, and there's a reason.

Back when I was in my army quarters, we often had salesmen knocking on the door, and most of them were con artists. I remember in Germany when my missus answered the door to a blind guy with one arm, he was selling pegs, he said he was a veteran. She took pity on him and purchased the pegs.

She came back into the lounge with her bag of pegs. 'How much did they set you back?' I said. 'Twenty DM.' '20 fucking Deutschmarks, for a packet of pegs.' Apparently, this was her third packet in two months, purchased while I was away on exercise. I walked her over to the window and there he was the so called one armed blind man getting his brand new Merc.

Buying a German schrank on finance was another big con; some of these were right monstrosities. It seemed like everyone had to have one. Yours had to be bigger and more expensive than your neighbours, talk about keeping up with the Jones'! I got one on finance, it took years to pay off. What was I thinking? And to go with your nice big scary if it falls on you it will kill you schrank, you needed a few original oil paintings, so your living room could look like a gothic museum.

German schrank

As soon as the schrank salesman had ripped you off, along came another salesman selling oil paintings. No doubt produced by some poor art student who was paid next to nothing. To be honest, I thought some of the paintings were really good, but expensive and nearly all of them were scenes of mountains and forests, they looked like where we'd been digging in for the past five years. That was the last scene I wanted to greet me when I arrived home from exercise.

They told you the paintings would be worth thousands in years to come when the student became the next Picasso, yeah alright. I left thirty odd years ago and

I've still got my fucking overdraft because of them, arseholes. I don't know where the picture went. I wonder if there is anybody out there that made a fortune on their painting.

The military should have done more to protect gullible twats like me. So that's why veterans hate salesmen unless you're a salesman veteran, then that's alright!

So, do what I do when one of these wankers comes knocking at your door. Tell them you were jerking off and they disturbed you, they'll leave, or they'll join in. Just make sure they are not girl guides. Another good one, answer the door naked wearing rubber gloves.

If I was a salesman, I'd sell no salesmen/soliciting signs. Now, that's an idea.

THE UNIFORM

ACTORS WEARING THE UNIFORM

Don't you just hate it when it comes to war films, when actors think they can just jump into a uniform. To a civvy they'll get away with it every time. For a veteran they all look like complete and utter cockwombles, bad Walts, no that's being disrespectful to Walts.

Take the film Wild Geese. It was a cracking film. For me, what let it down were the shocking berets, they all should have been charged for crimes against beret shaping. Oh, and then there's the big shiny targets, cap badges and the brand new crisp uniforms in the battle scenes. As if....

'What the fuck is that on your fucking head?'

They spend millions on these films. There is an easy fix to the problem, why don't they hire veterans to tell them they all look like cunts? An ex guards RSM would be good. 'You, yes you, you overpaid piece of shit, what the fuck is that you are wearing on your head?'

CARRY ON WALTING

As the time of year approaches the 11th November, maximum Walt activity begins. Many veterans will gather in the towns and cities across the land to attend the remembrance parades. It can be a long day as the veterans stand there for hours, sometimes in the pouring rain, to honour the fallen and rightly so. What else is there to do but do a little Walt spotting?

All you Walt commandos out there, wearing your gongs and bling, if you're not on the ball and haven't done your homework, you will be outed. It's amazing how far these Walter Mitty's will go to live out their fantasies!

There are all sorts of Walt types out there. Don't ask me why the sad fucks do it! Some are really good at it, but some are an embarrassment to Walting. Come on guys, if you're going to Walt, make a fucking effort some of you.

Here are a few tips that might help you get through the day.

TATTOO'S

An SAS tattoo is not a good idea. For one, members of the Special Forces wouldn't go around advertising it and two, if you are a Walt and have already got a Special Forces tattoo, don't have it next to your Mickey Mouse tattoo, it's a bit of a giveaway.

DID YOU KNOW?

The word tattoo for designs on the skin originates

from the Tahitian word tatau and was introduced to Britain by seamen who had been on Captain Cook's voyage to Polynesia.

BRAVO 2 ZERO

Read some of Andy McNab's books or similar, but make sure you liaise with your Walt friends. You don't want to use the same stories if confronted.

RUMBLED

If you are close to getting rumbled, I suggest that you say something like you once had a rather serious bang on the head and, sometimes, your memory is a bit wanting. It's probably true anyway!

THE BALCONY

Never say you were first on the balcony, every Walt says that. Say you were the bloke holding the ladder! Or the guy who did the MacDonald's run when you got back.

CALL OF DUTY

You must complete at least two Call of Duty games. It will be tough, and it will mean some late nights, but stick with it. Never three it could cause you to suffer with PTSD.

IMPRESS THE LADIES

If you've chosen to Walt purely to impress the ladies and the mission is to get your end away, then go for it. I think most veterans would allow that, as long as, you get the beers in. Ultimately, if it gets you laid, why not! But don't try that in a garrison town. The quickest way to get a good looking girl to disappear, is to tell her that you're in the Army, you're more likely to end up with someone resembling the creature from the deep.

TRAINING AIDS

No need for military training, but I would advise you to watch the following films and try and pick up a few tips. It will give you that feeling you've been there and done it. The Guns of Navarone, Kelly's Heroes, A Bridge too Far, The Longest Day, Apocalypse Now, The Matrix, Blazing Saddles, The Desert Song, Finding Nemo and Mary Poppins.

REMEMBRANCE DAY

Once you get through your parade, my advice is not to stay for the piss up. Being exposed as a Walt by three hundred pissed up angry veterans, could be a bad move and have a lasting effect on your physical appearance.

CDM

Don't wear too many medals. Get them in the right order and make sure your gongs are protected. They could easily melt if it's a freak warm day. Take special care with your CDM from the 70s, the Cadburys dairy milk medal could be worth a few quid nowadays.

If you are a beginner Walt and haven't any medals yet, before you go trawling eBay, there is good news if you were born in 1928, the same year Mickey was created. You might be entitled to the Mickey Mouse

Watch Decoration. Very unlikely though, as that would put you in your 90's.

CHOOSE THE BEST

If you do get asked what mob you were in and stuff, some Walts say the SAS or make up some random fictional unit like the SOANBRRRDT - Special Operations Amphibious Naval Boat Rescue, Response and Reconnaissance Development Team. Be warned, that might lead to some tricky questions. Don't hit the panic button, though, you can always fall back on the 'I can't really say, I'm tied under the Official Secrets Act, sorry.' My advice is if you're going to Walt then say you were a cook, or something a little less dramatic, and anyway military cooks have killed far more people than the SAS over the years.

STANDARDS

Walt attacking a Walt is rare, but not unheard of. If you see any pathetic attempts at Walting go for it, be a proud Walt, out them, they give proper Walt's a bad name!

THE HEAT OF BATTLE

Most military personnel never talk about what they did 'in the heat of battle' but they will tell you about how cheap the whores were in Belize and Berlin. Or when they blew up a camel in desert storm. My advice is that you don't go down the road of 'I remember slotting a load of the Taliban in Afgan.' Walt alert will start ringing in their heads.

RAPID PROMOTION

Being a Walt has its perks. If you think you deserve a promotion, go ahead promote yourself, a little rapid promotion won't hurt, L/Cpl to Sergeant Major, Lieutenant-Colonel to Major-General or even Field Marshal all in three years. Remember, for Ex Officers the head dress changes to bowler hat. Good luck, Sir! And last of all we'll be looking out for you!

But the best piece of advice I can give is don't do it, you are stealing someone else's valour.

HOW TO SIMULATE ARMY LIFE

Want to be a soldier, but really don't want to commit precious years of your life? Or you've been out for a while now and you want to remember what it's like being back in again. Don't worry, it's common, we've all been there. Here are some easy ways to simulate exactly what it's like to be a soldier.

Dig a hole in your garden and live in it for two weeks. Set up the sprinklers to spray you with cold water every hour. Check the perimeter every night at midnight. Set your alarm clock to go off at random times during the night to practice your stand to. Dig a shit pit behind the shed. Make sure the smell carries to your neighbour's house.

Every Thursday night dress up in your best clobber, drown yourself in Old spice or Brute and head for the local bingo hall and grab yourself a granny. (Don't forget your dabbers). Take advantage of the £1 a pint happy hour offer, between the early session and main session. Then head home, using your kebab compass.

Sit on the bog for hours reading the grot mags you've been hiding behind the cistern and don't come out until you've drawn a cock on the wall.

Don't bother showering or changing your socks for a few weeks.

Once the missus has made the beds, randomly during the day tear the blankets off and shout 'this is not fucking good enough,' repeat a number of times for no reason.

Routinely take all household appliances apart, clean them and put them back together, even if they haven't been used.

Empty the rubbish bins all over your house at weekends, then make sure it's all clean again for Monday morning.

Wake the whole street up every morning at 0600 hours for area cleaning.

Fill a backpack with fifty pounds of kitty litter. Put it on your back for twenty-four hours and jog everywhere.

Hard targeting down to the corner shop.

Blindfold your missus and make her give you a haircut

with the garden shears. Then get her to sew big pockets to the legs of your trousers and never use them.

Paint your vehicle with camouflage paint.

Use random contents of the fridge to make range stew. Blindfold the brats, make them wait in line for at least an hour. Repeat daily, no matter how tired you are. Eat everything cold. Eat so fast you don't taste the food.

Get the missus to make you up a horror bag for work, Panda pop, sweaty cheese sandwiches, a five day old, boiled egg and a packet of plain crisps.

Get your neighbour to give you your mail at monthly intervals.

Place a barrier and sentry box on your driveway and make the brats stag on 2 on 4 off. Get them to inform you when your mother-in-law approaches, so you can head for your hole in the garden.

Tie a string to your foot that runs to your missus' foot, so she can tug on the string when the mother-in-law has gone, plus you can give her a tug when you want a brew. Maintain iPhone silence. And remember, if you have nothing to do, clean something that doesn't need cleaning.

Whilst on holiday at the seaside, instead of building sand castles practice your trench digging, etc.

YOU KNOW YOU'RE A VETERAN WHEN

You advise your brats to never join the army. Join the navy instead.

You've hurried to get somewhere, then waited around all day waiting for what you hurried for to hurry up and happen.

You still call people Sir.

Every sentence of yours contains at least one acronym.

Your stable belt doesn't fit anymore. It just props your beer belly up.

You say, 'say again' instead of 'pardon me?'

You're making a bed, it's hospital corners, always.

When people don't form an orderly line, you want to scream.

You don't use an umbrella and never will.

You turn into a drill Sergeant when you're on a family holiday.

You're able to find things in the dark.

You have to make a call to 999, it stops being a phone call and becomes a radio conversation... over.

You have a pocket full of nub ends.

You shave in the shower.

Your missus has to remind you, 'If you wear that combat jacket, you'll look like a Walt.'

You take a different route home each night.

You think a six-pack a night is 'normal.'

You've told the same story, seven different times, to the same people.

You take the wife on the ration run to Tesco.

You refer to those who haven't served as civvies, even though you are now a civvy.

Pay day comes around proper fags instead of roll ups.

You still call clip boards, Mill boards.

You refer to the cheap coffee as G10 coffee.

A sewing kit is a housewife.

A bed is a Pit.

Bosses are Rupert's.

You're not drunk you're shit faced.

You only ever need one piece of bog roll.

You can spark up a fag in gale force winds with no effort.

WARNING

GRUMPY OLD VETERAN

SIGNING OFF, TIME TO LEAVE

It affects people in different ways. Personally, I couldn't wait to leave and I've never really looked back until now. I knew the writing was on the wall when I started to get comments like 'Is that right Wardi? Did you do the first stag on Hadrian's Wall?' Cheeky sprog, at least my number's not the population of fucking China!

When you hear someone whinging about a bit of kit and how outdated, it is, but you can remember that bit of kit being the dog's bollocks, when it was first issued to you.

When you're on RSM's drill parade and he doesn't shout at you to get your hair cut....Because you don't have hair anymore... it's time to leave.

For others, it was a sad time, the military was all they knew and they were forced to leave. Made redundant, medical discharge, or their time was up. What the hell were they going to do now? A lot of my buddies went straight in the TA, joined the police, the prison service, security officers, etc. And some just walked out of the camp gates chucked their MOD 90 away and said. **'THANK FUCK THAT'S OVER WITH, NO MORE MILITARY FOR ME!'** Only to join back up again twelve months later, I've seen a few of them do that.

WHAT THE HELL HAPPENED TO YOU?

You might have been physically fit when you served. The PTI's made sure of that. It was part of the routine and culture to pass that BFT. You knew if you didn't, you'd get your arse kicked. Those reasons no longer exist, you're now a civvy.

Whatever shape you were in when you left, you'll find things start to go downhill pretty quickly. Guess what, those thoughts you had of living a long and healthy life start to fade when they have to compete with Doritos, beer, and Netflix. At least 60% of us become fat bastards.

Despite the years of reacting to by the left double march ten times round, my beautiful body go, and get over that fucking wall move. Most of us will end up on Facebook or at Remembrance Day when one of your veteran buddies catches up with you and says, 'What the hell happened to you? You fat cunt.' Then you look down at your belly and say, 'fuck he's right.'

Early morning runs, five miles, ten miles, fifteen miles, with what felt like a fridge on your back, and the odd assault course or two thrown in for good measure. Then, just when you thought 'look, there's the Bedford to take you back to camp,' you hear the tail gate dropping. Not a chance. That would be too easy, it was yet another fucking tab. Of course, not everyone got that treatment, it depended who you were with, the Para's and Marines, as we all know, are up there. But for most of us, we had our share. To think we did all that without any real issue or ailment. Were we super fit, or was it a myth? I think it was because we tried a lot harder than normal people. That might have something to do with getting our arses kicked, failure hurts.

STOP FUCKING WHINGING, YOU SIGNED UP FOR IT, I HEAR THEM SAY. BUT WE DIDN'T KNOW THIS WAS GOING TO HAPPEN.

Fast-forward thirty years. It's the 21st century, where is my robot, my flying car and laser gun I was promised when I was a brat? No chance. All you're left with is a body not fit for purpose, a fucking wreck, unless you're one of the super human lucky ones.

Cartilages fucked, worn joints, constant pain running through your knees, ankles, shoulders, and back... Thanks for that. Health and safety in the workplace? Do me a fucking favour. Did we get rewarded for all the bullshit? Of course we didn't. All we have are our memories. Memories of when we had a waistline, we read without glasses, shagged properly. When we didn't need to clip nostrils, ears, shoulder blades and neck, not having to hedge trim every bloody orifice. Go for a proper piss rather than in a bag or bottle.

DATING A VETERAN

You met online through a dating agency. You were well impressed with his profile; 'I love walking, travel, socialising and spending cosy nights in watching TV.'

What he really meant was 'I miss those 20k tabs carrying 40k on my back, arriving back from Afghanistan, getting shit faced with his buddies, then spending the rest of the weekend festering in his room watching porn from his pit.

If you are interested in dating a veteran, here is some advice.

If you're going to date a veteran, the first thing you should do is make sure you are on time. Nothing will piss a veteran off more than arriving late for dinner or a pre-determined activity.

Secondly, it's really important right at the beginning, you need to equip yourself with a dark sense of humour and quick. At first his sense of humour might come as a bit of a shock. For instance, you are having your first romantic meal together, it's going well. Then suddenly, he takes off his prosthetic leg and places it on the seat next to him. Instead of going into shock, you need to hit back with, for example 'At least you won't do a runner on me, will you luv.' Brilliant he'll like that, it's love at first bite. It doesn't matter if you've had more spunk than a guardroom mattress, you're his girl.

'Waiter... another menu please'

First date with a veteran: I love your sense of humour. After six months: Everything is a one big fucking joke

to you, isn't it?
Lead us not into temptation, just point us in the
general direction and we'll find it from there.

CONFUCIUS SAYS

To this day, sometimes I sit on my patio having a
beer, thinking, what the fuck was that all about? Some
of the things we did or were made to do, were just
mind boggling.

Like being issued a pickaxe handle at the guardroom
to protect yourself and your comrades from terrorist
attack.

Earning a good conduct medal for eighteen years of
undetected crime.

Sitting in a trench full of water all weekend for an
attack that never comes...

Sleeping for thirty minutes in a trench you spent all
night digging, only to fill it in again the next morning.

Patrolling the streets of Belfast worried about firing
back if someone shot at you. Would I be liable in
years to come?

Going Semi Tac surely you are, or you aren't?

Being paid to go to Cyprus for 6 months!

Being made to salute anything with the UN badges on
it, including UN dustbin lorries on sentry duty.

Finding out the Regiments future plans and who's

involved from the Missus via letter while on tour.

Kicking the shit out of each other over something stupid, then heading down the NAAFI that night, and end up buying each other a pint.

Picking up naturally occurring fallen leaves in the middle of autumn, because they somehow offend the RSM. Then being told by the RSM that you weren't quick enough. 'Report to the guardroom with exactly 2000 leaves at 2200 hours.'

Why did we have a Queens Birthday parade every year when she could never be arsed to turn up for them.

Why didn't the military order the boots without fucking pimples on them?

Getting up at 5.30 for a 9 o'clock start! All that time that I'll never get back.

Why was I always overdrawn at the bank, when I still had cheques left in my cheque book?

Working a twenty-four hour day and then being told you have to work another eight hours. Civvies aren't stupid enough to put up with it.

'Let the hill do the work.' I still don't understand that one.

Making sure you packed your PT kit into your large pack for exercises.

Not being able to recite Queen's Regulations, because it's against Queen's Regulations.

LIVING WITH A VETERAN

AFV RECOGNITION

Am I on my own or does anyone else still practice their AFV recognition? It impresses the grandkids, but it pisses the missus off big time.

I've been spotting ex-soviet armoured fighting vehicles ever since I left Germany in the 80's. I always remember one embarrassing moment. I was deeply engrossed in this war movie with the grandkids when I did the usual.

'You see that tank, that's a T72 Russian tank, that is.'
'Wow Granddad, you know everything', said my youngest. Then the Missus butts in saying;
'Not quite everything. I think you'll find that's a T64. It's got a gap between the third and fourth road wheels.'

I suppose all the years boring the tits off her listening to my AFV Recognition she took it all in.

I CORRUPTED MY MISSUS

When I met her, she was a sweet innocent girl. After moving into married quarters things started to change, she had made enormous progress in her swearing. I was surprised how quickly my gentle, quiet Sunday

School-attending missus learned to swear like a trooper.

By the time I left the military she became a grand master of profanity, obscenity and vulgarity. I remember when we went on our first holiday to Clacton in a caravan. We'd just got engaged and she bought me a gold Seiko watch as a present, it must have cost her a couple of weeks wages. I'd only had it thirty minutes when I lost it. I'd left it in the campsite shower block and her response was. 'It's ok, it doesn't matter, it's not the end of the world is it. I'll get you another one.'

For a start I wouldn't get a watch now, but if I did and I happened to lose it, I could not imagine what masterpieces of profanity she'd come up with now, and that's before I'd lost my testicles.

INTRUDERS

So, it's stupid o'clock in the morning and the Missus nudges me waking me up.

'I think there's someone downstairs' she says

'Ok, ok, I've got this' I say, still in that 30 second where the fuck am I zone.
'What the hell are you faffing about at? Go and see who's downstairs.'
'I can't find my rifle.'
'You haven't got a rifle, you're not in the army anymore.'
'You're right, I'm not, am I.'

I come to my senses, I reach down and arm myself with my weapon of choice, my three iron, zip ties and duct tape. It was either that or Walten Kommando mincing knife, or the huge double-ended Klingon sword I bought on eBay. I only use it if things really get serious.

KLINGON SWORD

My last resort is the Missus. She is enough of a deterrent, she'd frighten off any intruder; she scares the shit out of me. Anyway, whoever it is, if some scumbag breaks into my house violating my rights as a homeowner, when they enter my property, they leave their rights at the boundary.

I was on my way downstairs, in one hand, my three iron and my other hand over my right eye to conserve my night vision. I came face to face with this male figure slightly smaller than myself. I didn't challenge him I just swung my golf club and smashed.

Take that, you wanker! Then I found out I've just smashed my missus's brand new, full length mirror she bought earlier that day, she didn't tell me about it. Now I was in trouble I spent the rest of the night telling her 'put the Klingon sword down it was an accident.'

WALKING CALCULATOR

I'm always counting the number of paces it is to anywhere. When I get the chance, I like to practice my judging distance. The missus would say 'How far do you think TESCO's is from our house?'

Me: 'Approximately 675 metres.'
Missus: 'How the bloody hell do you know that?'
Me: 'It's built in, oh and it's on a bearing of 3300 mils, I say.'
Missus: 'Ok, you can shut up now, you're boring me.'

Another thing the Missus calls me the walking calculator. When we go shopping I'm able to estimate how much we've spent and only be a few pence out before we arrive at the checkout. It must have been something to do with all those choggie runs. I'm sure I'm not the only veteran who does this.

DID YOU KNOW?

The magnetic compass was first invented by the Chinese Han Dynasty around 206 BC. The compass was used in the Song Dynasty China by the military for navigation around 1040 and was used for maritime navigation by 1111. There are several different types of compass around today, amongst them the Silva compass and the officer's compass LONG DISTANCE COMPASS. The LDC compass automatically selects the longest route to a chosen destination, depending on the officer's rank.

I HAVE NO LIVE ROUNDS AND...

It's bonfire night and you find yourself putting on a bit of a firework display. You carry out the safety rules, like you're back on the ranges again, planning your firework display with military precision. All your fireworks (you call them pyrotechnics) are safely stored in that old ammo box. You read the instructions in full on every firework. Make sure all your guests are a safe distance, in that four-man trench you dug for the occasion earlier, and are given a full safety brief, actions on and all that.

Once the first firework goes off, you spend the rest of the night slagging them off saying shit like, 'Call that a bang. I remember when I was on the Falls road and that bomb went off'. 'Call that a banger. That's crap, we need a few thunder flashes around here.'

Before long, you've bored the pants off them that much they're wandering off inside. Then you look in your ammo box and you realise that some Muppet has nabbed the roman candles. 'Just a minute you lot, before you go I want you to make the necessary declaration I have... blah... blah... blah... when I come to you.' Too late, they're all inside tucking into your hot dogs and toffee apples leaving you to pick up the empties. When you have made the garden safe, you find out the bastards have locked the patio door.

IS IT EASE SPRINGS YET?

Do you ever sit outside a cafe and observe people and wonder, where the fuck am I? It's like being on another planet. As I take another sip from my £2.50 cup of tea and pull another pube out of my over-priced sandwich, I think to myself, is this the world we live in now, or is the problem me?

Here's a list of things I hate and a sure sign the dementia is setting in. Hold on a minute that old cunt across the room keeps staring at me! Oh, it's a mirror...

I still hate the sound of anything rattling when I go out anywhere. The Missus's handbag is shocking. Sometimes I make her jump up and down before we go shopping and have a go at her for putting too much face cam on. You need to break up the outline of your face I tell her.

Another one is Hollywood war stories, told by the Walts to gullible barmaids down your local. Special Forces my arse, special faeces more like.

People who bring screaming babies into supermarkets and pretend they can't hear them. Control the brat, for fuck's sake. All they need is a good hiding; it never did me any harm.

Saint Bob of Geldof, and his cronies trying to talk us into parting with our hard earned cash to give to African dictators so they can buy a new fleet of limo's and luxury villa's while their country starve. Feed the world? Feed my celebrity status more like. Oh, and that one fucking note piano player on nearly all the charity adverts.

Yelling down my mobile phone at my Missus telling her I can't find my mobile phone.

Going to Tesco's in my car which is only 675 metres away incidentally, walking back, then later looking out the window, wondering where my car has gone.

I've been out for a long time now and I'm still waiting for this, 'I'm on leave' feeling to go away.

TAT

Being a crusty old veteran, over the years I've turned into a bit of a hoarder. I've got tat everywhere and most of it is worthless, apart from my collection of Readers wives. They were proper WANK MAGS, they were.

Most of the tat is the old lady's; old tea sets, knitting patterns her mum gave her from the 60's. Her mum, bless her heart, also gave her that old post war austerity mind-set of, 'don't throw it out. It might come in useful one day.' It never was by the way. Apart from that ugly vase, that came crashing down on my bonce one night for eyeing up the barmaid in the Dog and Duck.

Now all our brats have flown the nest, and just popping in now and again to see if we're still alive. All the accumulated tat needs to go. Hundreds of paperbacks, old pay slips, old army surplus, Blue Peter annuals, forty years of clothes we'd kept, thinking and hoping we'd get back into them again, but never did, old Christmas trees, VHS video's all destined for the skip, job done.

I'm sure the mice and other rodents living amongst it all will appreciate the change of diet. I didn't extend mass clear out to the loft. Main reason, I can't climb up there anymore. The brats can fight over that lot when I kick the bucket. Let them run the risk of being killed in an avalanche of accumulated shite. Anyway, there's so much crap up there, the insulation properties of it must be saving us a fortune, keeping the heating bill down.

The money we must have wasted over the decades on utter rubbish is enough to make me weep. Talk about heating the house. I suppose I could have an accidental house fire. Save the really valuable stuff, oh and the Readers Wives and bank the insurance cheque. A trip to Benidorm is on the cards I think!

I lost my sense of smell years ago, but some smells you never forget.

HERE ARE 10 SMELLS YOU'LL NEVER FORGET

1. The smell of wet jersey heavy wool, after drill parade.
2. The smell of old cam nets.

3. The smell of burning boot polish, when you were running out.

4. The smell of a hot GPMG barrel after firing.

5. The smell of the CS gas residue lingering on your noddy suit, it could clear the sinuses and a hangover... Just like that.

6. The smell of Bacon Grill for the first time.

7. The smell of hot mud cooling on the exhaust of your APC, after a blast across Soltau.

8. The smell of ironed starch.

9. The rancid smell of the fermenting swill bin in the cook-house.

10. The smell of wet cow pats after you've dived head first into a firing position.

As I grow older and my hearing begins to fail, certain sounds bring back memories of years gone by.

HERE ARE 10 SOUNDS YOU'LL NEVER FORGET

1. The sound of the rattle of the cattle grid on entering the Sennybridge training area.

2. The sound of the perfect Present Arms on RSM'S drill parade. Nailed it. I'm going home this weekend.

3. The sound of a GPMG on SF Mode. Better than the sound of a Ferrari engine.

4. The sound of some twat brushing his boots at

sparrow fart o'clock, while everybody else was still in their pits trying to get another five minutes.

5. The sound and joy on hearing the magic words "ENDEX."

6. The sound of the crack and thump.

7. The sound of contact wait out, comes over the radio.

8. The sound of firing the SLR on gas setting 0.

9. The sound of the base drum on drill parade.

10. The sound of birds chirping at stand to.

I'll never forget my army number, eight digits etched into my brain that even the darkest depths of Alzheimer's will probably never erase.

When I hear a Military band strike up.... I stand up, push my chest out, suck in my ten-bellies, hold my head up and start swinging those arms, and think back to those golden years, back when I was a young soldier again.... Then the nurse tells me to sit down because I'm upsetting everyone and gives me another injection. Cow, I need to organise that escape committee.

It can be fun being old, though! Holding up queues is my favourite pastime, pissing off all the young brats behind me as I pretend to struggle to find the right money, then say 'Oh, I haven't got enough, I'll have to pay by credit card' then pulling out my bus pass, 'is that it, I ask?' The frustration on their faces is priceless when you start looking in all your pockets at least three times holding up the queue even longer. I only came in for one onion and a bottle of GO-LESS to stop me pissing.

Yes, I would give my right testicle to be twenty again. I'm still twenty something in my mind and intend to squeeze as much out of life as I can. Have fun. Life is what you make it.

'Old soldiers never die, they simply fade away.'

The problem is that unless you end up as a name on a memorial somewhere we are all doomed to be civvies in the end. Lest we forget.

When I die, bury me upside down, so the world can KISS MY ARSE.

GLOSSARY

AFV – Armoured Fighting Vehicle

AWOL- Absent without Leave

BAOR – British Army of the Rhine

BFT – Battle Fitness Test

Blanco – A compound used to clean and colour webbing

Choggie – An independent snack shop

CO – Commanding Officer

Dhobi – Washing your kit

Egg Banjo – Fried Egg Sandwich

Fag – Cigarette

FUBAR – Fucked Up Beyond All Repair

Hard Targetting – Continuous Movement

KFS – Knife, Fork and Spoon

OC – Officer Commanding

PVR – Premature Voluntary Release

QM – Quarter Master

Queen's Parade – Breakfast

Recce – Reconnaissance

RSM – Regimental Sergeant Major

Schrank – A German Wall Unit

Semi- Tac – Not Fully Alert

Shell Scrape – A Large Hole

Shreddies – Underpants

Skint – Without Funds

SLR – Rifle

Smash – Powdered Potato

Swamped – Wet Yourself

Tabbing – Moving from one place to another

Walt – Walter Mitty. Someone who pretends to have served in the Military

ENDEX 2 UNCUT

ABOUT THE AUTHOR

After leaving the Army in 1988 Clive started a publishing company with a friend, publishing Adult and children's comics and had immediate success. Sadly, the success didn't last forever. With the introduction of Lads Magazines, adult comics and children's comics were on the decline, so in 2000 he took up a full-time job, but didn't give up writing whenever he could, writing sitcoms, stage plays, creating greeting cards and children's books.

Now with the digital age upon us he thought "Let's Get Digital." He has turned his old sitcoms, stage plays and ideas into books with encouraging results. He gets great pleasure from writing and writes as often as he can. Clive lives in Derbyshire with his wife Elaine, who is also a writer.

31121748R00069

Printed in Poland
by Amazon Fulfillment
Poland Sp. z o.o., Wrocław